Let Not Your Heart Be Troubled

Let Not Your Heart Be Troubled

RANDY MAXWELL

Pacific Press® Publishing Association
Nampa, Idaho
Oshawa, Ontario, Canada
www.pacificpress.com

Edited by Jerry D. Thomas
Cover Illustration by Lars Justinen
Design by Justinen Creative Group Inc.™

Additional copies of this book may be purchased online at
http://www.adventistbookcenter.com

ISBN 0-8163-1915-4

02 03 04 05 06 • 5 4 3 2 1

To Dani, my littlest angel.

Remember:

"Life is difficult.
God is Merciful.
Heaven is sure."

Other Books by Randy Maxwell

On Eagles' Wings
Loving Is Fundamental
If My People Pray
Bring Back the Glory
5 Steps to Christlike Living

Contents

You will not fear the terror of night,
nor the arrow that flies by day,
nor the pestilence that stalks in the darkness,
nor the plague that destroys at midday.

—*Psalm 91:5, 6*

1

Let not your heart be troubled . . .

By Terror

My daughter makes me cry. Because I have three daughters, I had better be more specific. Danielle, my youngest, makes me cry. It's not that she's bad or gets into trouble. She's innocent and gets into my heart.

On September 11, 2001, terrorists hijacked four commercial airliners and flew them into the World Trade Center towers in Manhattan and into the Pentagon, killing thousands of innocent men, women, and children. And just as our minds were trying to wrap around the horrific scene of flames and acrid smoke belching from gaping holes in those 110-story monuments to American might and achievement, the unthinkable happened. They collapsed.

At the publishing company where I work, we tried, unsuccessfully, to concentrate on our duties. But with each update on the latest attack—the crash in rural Pennsylvania, the collapse first of tower two, then tower one—my gut twisted into a tighter knot, squeezing more and more bitter acid up my throat and into my mouth. It was the blackest day this country had ever faced, and the horror of it shook us all to our knees.

It was the blackest day this country had ever faced.

My kids were in school that day. Naturally, they were affected. The TV news was beamed into their classrooms and they witnessed again and again and again from every conceivable angle the planes, with innocent passengers aboard, slamming into those buildings. They witnessed the towers pancaking and disappearing in volcano-like plumes of smoke and ash . . . again and again and again. And for my daughters, who have a daddy who flies often, the impact was devastating.

Calls to my wife who works at the Christian school my daughters attend confirmed what I knew they must be feeling. They were terrified and weren't eating.

When I got home that evening, everyone was walking

around in a daze and a palpable feeling of dread hung heavily in the air. I gathered the family in the living room for prayer. I knew my children's sense of security and well-being had been torpedoed with the same force as the World Trade Center had been torpedoed hours earlier.

I don't know if it came through in my voice, but inside I was shaking. I opened the Scriptures and did what fathers are supposed to do—I led my family to the throne of grace for help and comfort in our time of need. I turned to Psalm 91 and read those immortal words of comfort:

Surely he will save you from the fowler's snare
and from the deadly pestilence.
He will cover you with his feathers,
and under his wings you will find refuge;
his faithfulness will be your shield and rampart.
You will not fear the terror of night,
nor the arrow that flies by day,
nor the pestilence that stalks in the darkness,
nor the plague that destroys at midday.
A thousand may fall at your side,
ten thousand at your right hand,
but it will not come near you. . . .
If you make the Most High your dwelling—
even the Lord, who is my refuge—

then no harm will befall you,
no disaster will come near your tent.
For he will command his angels concerning you
to guard you in all your ways (vv. 3-11).

I then turned to the words of Jesus and read His own account of what life would be like just before He comes again. I was attempting, through scripture, to reestablish our faith as a family in God and in the hope of a better world beyond the one that was reeling beneath us at that moment.

The kids were quiet; their young faces grim with worry. Danielle was curled up on her mother's lap in nearly a fetal position.

It happened about the time I started mentioning prayer for the families of those who were lost in the attacks. Suddenly, Dani couldn't hold back the dam of emotion any longer. Her eight-year-old face twisted in pain. Her mouth opened and quiet sobs began to spill out. Instantly I felt hot tears spring to my own eyes, momentarily blurring my vision. A pang of agony stabbed my chest like a knife and I had to look away to maintain my composure. Until that moment, I hadn't cried. As awful as that day had been, I hadn't shed tears. But the sight of my youngest child weeping in sympathy for the victims and in fear for her safety and that of her family, got to me.

Dads are supposed to make their children feel safe and

secure. On September 11 I realized how difficult it would be to do that from that day forward.

A week and a half later, she got to me again. On the morning I wrote these very words, I was headed to the garage to get in my car and drive to the airport. This was to be my first flight since the tragedy and emotions were running high. Everyone was trying their best to be brave and not say what they were thinking. No one needed to say anything.

We had just had prayer as a family and, in keeping with our custom whenever someone leaves on a trip, we hugged and gave each other "blessings" in the name of the Lord. (See Numbers 6:24-27.) As I went to hug and bless Danielle, I noticed her long face. I could tell she was struggling with her fears. I had held her close and kissed her forehead in reassurance, but as I reached the pantry, I worried about my little girl. How I wanted to assure her that everything was going to be alright. And that's when she got me again.

Before I could get out the door, Dani slipped up behind me and thrust a piece of paper in my line of sight. "Here, Daddy," she said soberly. "Look at it when you're on the plane."

"OK, Sweetheart," I replied. *Whoosh!* As quickly as she came, she was gone. I turned the paper over and looked down on a drawing that spoke volumes. In the simple style of an eight-year-old, was a drawing of me with luggage in my hands, and standing next to me a smiling angel, my guardian and companion.

Once again I felt a lump in my throat and a sting in my eyes. My Dani wanted to reassure me that I was not going to be alone on my flight—God and His angels were going to be with me. Her simple message to me that morning is the message I want to bring you in the pages of this little book: When troubles come—as they surely will—you are not alone; God is with you.

When troubles come—as they surely will—you are not alone; God is with you.

"Let not your heart be troubled," Jesus said to His disciples. "You believe in God, believe also in me" (John 14:1, KJV). But how are we to do this? With scenes of unspeakable horror permanently etched into the memory chips in our brains; with the economic stability of our nation teetering on the brink of collapse; with the relatively carefree lifestyle that we Americans have always enjoyed (and taken for granted) becoming a thing of the past, how are we to relate to these words of Jesus? Even as we grieve and our hearts ache with pain, how do we not let our hearts be "troubled"?

I wrote these words from seat 13B on Horizon flight #2391 from Boise to Seattle. The date was September 21—the day after President Bush readied the nation for war in a historic joint session of Congress. I wondered how I would feel. I anticipated a miserable flight—miserable with my own apprehensions and imaginings of a terrorist in every seat. But you know what? That angel that my daughter drew on paper was real. Instead of dread, I felt a peace that passed understanding. And though a young high schooler was sitting next to me in 13A, I knew who else was right beside me.

For the next few pages I want us to be a family and gather around the Word of God as my family did the night of September 11. I want to revisit some of the more profound statements of assurance made by Jesus, David, and the apostle Paul—statements that will anchor our faith and help us regain our bearings in the midst of this storm we call life. Why? Because believers get shaken too. We have questions. We doubt. We fear. We also grieve and hurt. But we've also been given incredible spiritual truths and perspectives on life that if taken to heart, will be a shelter in the time of storm.

I need to know how to live with confidence and peace when the inexplicable happens.

So do you.

I need to know that Jesus hasn't left me alone when I feel like a two-year-old who's gotten separated from his mommy in a crowded shopping mall.

So do you.

I need to know how I'm supposed to live in and above this crazy world that can be so full of joy one moment and so full of pain the next.

So do you.

I need Jesus.

Again.

And again.

And again.

So do you.

Our need is our passport into the presence of God. He's waiting for us to come. Jesus wants to hold us close and reorient our spiritual and emotional compasses so we feel assured—again—

that He is in control, and there is no need to fear.

Trouble comes in many forms, not just in the silhouette of an airplane over a city skyline. Marriages dissolve, loved ones get cancer, jobs are terminated, children rebel, aging parents must be cared for, wars, famines, and plagues take the lives of many. How do we make it through with our faith intact? The way we always have—on our knees holding the Word of God in one hand, and grasping hold of a smiling angel with the other.

If you're in need of an anchor today, keep reading . . . and hold on.

❖

Lord, I need to know that You are still in control. Intellectually, I know this is true, but everything seems so out of control right now. Fear is a constant, and unwelcome, companion. I know I'm not supposed to put my trust in anything other than You, least of all anything in this world. But times of trouble expose who I really am and reveal where I've placed my trust. Please be my refuge from the storm. Anchor my soul in your Word and teach me how to hold on to You and not let go. Amen.

All that pleases is but for a moment.

All that troubles is but for a moment.

Nothing is important except that which is eternal.

—Inscriptions over three cathedral doors in Milan

2

Let not your heart be troubled . . .

About This World

I went home recently. Not where I live right now, but home to Los Angeles where I was born and spent the first twenty-eight years of my life. I was in "the Southland" to speak at a large prayer rally, and, after landing at LAX, I decided to revisit my old stomping grounds and take a nostalgic drive down memory lane. (Actually, the drive was down Imperial highway, but that doesn't sound nearly as romantic.)

My first stop was 10932 Wilkie Ave., in Inglewood—the address of my boyhood home. It looked so familiar, yet so different. There, above the garage, was the basketball hoop where I played so many imaginary championship games. Memorable battles between larger-than-life superstars, in which I played all the roles. I smiled as I thought of the "home runs" I used to hit using a broom stick to knock chunks of decorative landscaping bark over the house from backyard to front. I had flashbacks of me riding my brand-new, gold, three-speed bike with the metal-flake banana seat and chrome "sissy bar" up and down the sidewalk in front of the house.

The new owners had painted the California-style stucco house a different color—bluish grey instead of the light yellow I remembered. But the lawn was still neatly manicured and the neighborhood in general still looked good. So many happy memories there.

But I couldn't go in and get a soda out of the fridge, or shoot a game of 8-ball on my dad's pool table, or play "Pong" on my kid brother's Atari video game system. None of those things was there anymore. Though I lived in that house for ten years, it was no longer my home. It was someone else's now.

Next, I found an old burger place my wife and I used to go to on Saturday nights when we were teenagers. Nothing had changed. Same tables. Same menu. Same umbrella-shaped light fixtures. (From the look of those lights, it appeared that they hadn't been dusted since my wife and I were there the last time!)

I ordered the "usual" and replayed mental videos of Suzette and me sitting in those same chairs more than twenty years ago. I remembered the time she accidentally jammed her big toe underneath the glass door that I was sitting in front of at that very moment. Ahhh, such great memories.

It was the same place where I had spent so much time, but things weren't the same. I was twenty years older, my waist was at least six inches wider, and my sweetie was about 850 miles away in Idaho. A lot had remained the same, but a lot had changed too.

After collecting my order, I got back in the rental car and pointed it east on Imperial toward Lynwood where I went to school from grades 1-12. Suzette and I must have worn grooves in the asphalt with our tires over the years going back and forth between my home in Inglewood and hers in Lynwood. How many times had I driven this seven-mile stretch of road either in my own car, or riding Bus #3 or #4 in elementary school!

There was the fish market in Nickerson Gardens. The intersection at Mona Street where the generator light on our VW came on and we prayed for the Lord to keep the engine running until we could get to a safer part of town. Coming up were the railroad tracks on Ferndale Road where Suzette's front axle on her Ford Galaxy 500 (affectionately called "The Tank") broke and she nearly skidded off the road into a metal fence. A policeman said she was lucky. We knew she was blessed. I breathed a short prayer of thanks to God for sparing her as I drove past the spot.

Finally I arrived at what was once my school—Lynwood Academy. But long gone was the huge WWI-era airplane hanger that served as our auditorium. Gone were the beautiful Eucalyptus trees that once lined the driveways into the grounds. Gone was the playground where I spent many happy years as an elementary school student playing flag football, soccer, and chasing the girls on the monkey bars. (The truth is, they were chasing me!)

Squatting on top of my school grounds was a cement and glass montrocity that totally erased all memory of what had been. This behemoth, this intruder, was the new Lynwood High School that the city built after winning an eminent domain case against my church school. How dare they mess with my childhood!

I drove onto the Harris Street side where the entrance to the academy had been. Nothing was left of the tree-lined manicured lawns that used to grace the property and blended so well with the surrounding neighborhood. The "intruder" had taken everything. Or had it? I headed to the one spot where there might have been a remnant—a tiny shred of my past still visible. I stopped the car in front of where the main building had been and opened my door. I peered at the pavement below and let out a whoop of joy and clapped my hands. There it was! Something remained.

It had been a long standing tradition at Lynwood for the senior class to paint their class logo on the street in front of the main entrance. There, barely visible now from weather and years of street traffic, were flecks and splotches of paint left behind from the last logo that had been painted there.

"Ha!" I said as if someone was listening to me. "They couldn't take it all! Lynwood still lives!"

On I drove, to my wife's house where we had our first kiss, and later, our daughter Candice had her first birthday party. It looked so small now. This had been my second home, and the place we would usually stay when we would come back to California for a visit. But Suzette's mother had passed away, and we had sold the house. It belonged to someone else now. I didn't belong there either.

On to Downey, and to the Cheltham Arms apartments where Suzette and I lived for the first eight years of our marriage. Again I was amazed at how small it looked! I got out of the car and walked right up to the doors of Apartments L and D—the two places where we had lived. I could picture Suzette holding baby Candice in front of the door the day we brought her home from the hospital. But I didn't knock, and I didn't have a key. My name was no longer on the mailbox. The Maxwells didn't live here any longer.

Later that weekend, as I fought the traffic on the 5 and 10 freeways from the White Memorial Church in East L.A., en route to my aunt's home in the West Hollywood area, I had an epiphany. "Lord," I said aloud. "This is how you want us to live in this world, isn't it? I'm home. These places that I've been to are all familiar to me. I grew up here. I know these streets and these freeways like the back of my hand. But this is not my home. Though I have friends and relatives in this city, I am still a guest when I come to town. I have no place here to call my own. No place where I have my own key, my own recliner (with fugitive popcorn kernels wedged between the cushions), my own bathroom, or my own king-size bed that our kids like to camp out in on Friday nights and watch 'Veggie Tales.'

"I used to live in L.A., but this is *not* my home. My home is where my wife and children are—where my heart is. My home is in Idaho—that's where I belong."

And that's the point. Home *is* where the *heart* is. Where is your heart? Where are your energies, your focus, your enthusiasm and your priorities? Where have you fixed your affections? What does your list of short and long-term goals consist of? Does the list have a decidedly "earthly" flavor?

Jesus wants our hearts. He said, " 'Where your treasure is,

there your heart will be also' " (Matthew 6:21). Your "treasure" is what you esteem, value, and cherish. If the things you value and are willing to sacrifice to get are all of this world, you're in danger of forgetting where home is. " 'Do not store up for yourselves treasures on earth, where moth and rust [let's add disease, disaster, old age, accident, and hatred] destroy,' " said Jesus, " 'and where thieves break in and steal; but store up for yourselves treasures in heaven, where moth and rust do not destroy, and where thieves do not break in and steal.' " (Matthew 6:19, 20) In other words, don't leave your heart in the rental car in McDermitt, Nevada. (Trust me. You just want to get some gas and throw down some grub in McDermitt. You *do not* want to stay there!)

In the World; Not of It

My visit to southern California provided me with a new understanding of the phrase "Be *in* the world, but not *of* the world." I was *in* L.A., but not *of* it. I was "home" and yet not *at* home. I was "occupying" till my plane came to take me home, in the same way we're to occupy till Jesus comes (see Luke 19:13) to take us home.

We live here on this troubled planet. It is familiar to us. It's all we know. We live and love and work and die here. We go to school, get married, birth children, play sports, get sick, and build houses here. But this isn't our real home. This isn't where we're supposed to put down roots and stake a claim.

But sometimes we forget. Even as we sing our hymns and talk about heaven, we mistake this world for home. How does this happen?

For those of us living in the United States, things are pretty good even in tough times. We enjoy the highest standard of living on earth. Why should we be anxious to leave? Even the Hebrew exiles in ancient Persia had a hard time leaving for the homeland when allowed to return. Some stayed right where they were. They had settled in on foreign soil and had started to enjoy their new way of life. They had established lucrative businesses, plush Persian homes, and very comfortable lifestyles.

Like life in the Persian Empire, life here can be pretty good. But every now and then we are reminded that this is not home—that we are still on enemy territory; that evil does exist. Despite the appearance of prosperity and the "good life" we typically enjoy, we're all passengers on a hijacked aircraft called Earth that hurtles through space at thousands of miles an hour en route to certain destruction. The grave is the final destination for all of us, and though we fool ourselves into thinking we can cheat the grim reaper with the "Oil of

✤

Technology and science still has not found a cure for death.

Delay," tummy tucks, liposuction, hair plugs, implants, etc., apart from Christ, dust is still our destiny. Technology and science have still not found a cure for death.

WHY SO MUCH TROUBLE?

Why do we live with trouble? Because that's where we live! Jesus said, " 'In this world you will have trouble' " (John 16:33). There it is! We live on planet Trouble. It's capital is Rebellion. The ruling parties of its Congress are Suffering and Sorrow. The Supreme Court on planet Trouble stands on a platform of Injustice, and the president is Satan himself.

I don't have to tell you that bad things happen on planet Trouble. You've seen it on CNN, heard it on the radio, read about it in the paper, and experienced it first hand in your living room, on your block, and in your office. No one escapes. Everyone gets touched by trouble. From the Gaza Strip to Northern Ireland; from Bosnia to Ethiopia; from the Sudan to South Central L.A.; and from Afghanistan to lower Manhattan, trouble never takes a holiday.

On a recent trip to Anchorage, a guest singer from Maryland who works full time as a middle school principal, told me about a twelve-year-old girl he had sent home on a half-day suspension for fighting. When she got home, the girl invited five friends to her house, one of whom brought a loaded 357 magnum.

Somehow, the girl got shot in the chest. The blast blew a hole right through her body and took everything in her chest out through the exit wound in the back. Why do awful things like this happen? Because this world is NOT our home. Get that through your head. In the kingdom of this world, things like this happen. In the kingdom of heaven, things like this are no more.

And yet, despite the trouble, I still find myself clinging tenaciously to this place. Like many abusive marriages, the world dishes out repeated painful blows and threatens to destroy me and everything and everyone I hold dear. But I refuse to let the "Authorities" of heaven intervene. Life here may be hell, but it's all I know. It's sick, but it's familiar. Besides, the world isn't *that* bad all the time, right?

If this sounds a lot like denial, that's because it is. And when a person is in denial about their problem, be it drugs, alcohol, or abuse, they don't want help. They adapt to misery and make peace with pain. Left to their own devices, they will continue to make a home of havoc.

At times like this, a family intervention is needed.

The Intervention of Lot

Remember the story of Lot? Lot, a nephew of the patriarch Abraham had settled in the city of Sodom—a city known for its wickedness. Homosexual gang rape seemed to be the town pastime. (See Genesis 19:4-9.) Besides sexual violence, Sodom was " ' "arrogant, overfed and unconcerned; they did not help the poor and needy" ' " (Ezekiel 16:49). God was ready to put an end to this cesspool of unrighteousness, but first, He needed to get "His people" out, so He sent two angels to Sodom to evacuate Lot and his family before torching the place.

When the angels arrived, they found Lot "sitting in the gateway of the city" (Genesis 19:1). This is significant because traditionally, city fathers gathered at the gates or entrance to the town, to make important decisions. Lot's presence suggests that he was more than just a resident of Sodom, he was a leader in the community—perhaps a member of the city council! His entanglement with the customs, policies, and values of Sodom made it difficult for him to leave it all behind and get aboard the rescue chopper when the angels offered it. Despite the fact that Lot found himself in the unconscionable position of actually offering his two virgin daughters to be gang raped by the townspeople in order to protect the heavenly visitors, it still took some strongarm tactics on the part of the angels to pry Lot and his family from their beloved home.

"With the coming of dawn, the angels urged Lot, saying, 'Hurry! Take your wife and your two daughters who are here, or you will be swept away when the city is punished.' When he hesitated, the men grasped his hand and the hands of his wife and of his two daughters and led them safely out of the city, for the Lord was merciful to them" (Genesis 19:15, 16).

Despite the immorality and dangers of the place, Lot didn't want to let Sodom go. He had forgotten where "home" was and had put down roots in the wrong place. Lot escaped, but his wife didn't. Her heart belonged to Sodom and when she looked back, she indicated that she was one with the people there and shared their fate.

Jesus urged His disciples to " 'remember Lot's wife' "! (Luke 17:32) as a warning against becoming too attached to this world in light of His second coming. Are we remembering Lot's wife today? Is this world too much with us? Despite the immorality and dangers of the place, are we, like Lot, reluctant to let planet Trouble go? I confess that sometimes I am. Instead of traveling light here, my "checked baggage" and "carry-on's" seem to get heavier and more awkward the longer I stay.

And sometimes, out of love, God helps us lighten our load. Please understand. God doesn't cause the trouble that comes into our lives, but sometimes He permits it to shake us, so we'll loosen our grip on this world and turn our hearts toward home.

Going home

We were running late. I had never been in Australia before and I wanted to see so many things. But I had a plane to catch and time was not my friend. As my van driver scurried us across the Sydney Harbor Bridge, he said with urgency, "You just *have* to see the city before you go!"

I calmly corrected him. "The only thing I *have* to do is make my flight for home." And I meant it. Given the time, there was a lot of things I could enjoy doing. But I wasn't going to let sightseeing interfere with getting home.

If we don't get too distracted trying to look at all the "sights" this decaying world has to offer, we'll make certain that we don't miss our flight for home.

❖

Lord, I admit that this world is too much with me. In the best of times it seems my greatest desire is for what I can achieve or acquire here. The next promotion, my next house, a new car, or the next "sure thing" investment seem to occupy my thoughts, take my energy, and direct my actions. It's not that these things in and of themselves are "bad," but I find myself getting too comfortable here. I wish it didn't take trouble to cause me to remember that I'm still on foreign soil. But I'm still too much like Lot. Still tied emotionally to the things I've grown to love and lust after here.

Create within me a homesickness for heaven, Lord, that will help me to enjoy my brief layover here, without wanting to make it my final destination. I don't want to be so heavenly minded that I'm no earthly good, but neither do I want to be so earthly minded that I lose my focus and forget my purpose in being here. Thank you for the reminder, and for the roadmap home. Amen

Do not lose heart.

Though outwardly we are wasting away,

yet inwardly we are being renewed day by day.

For our light and momentary troubles

are achieving for us an eternal glory

that far outweighs them all.

So fix [your] eyes not on what is seen,

but on what is unseen.

For what is seen is temporary,

but what is unseen is eternal.

—2 Corinthians 4:16-18

3

Let not your heart be troubled . . .

By Circumstances

I've been behind bars before. Several times, in fact. No, I wasn't there to serve time. I was there to sing.

"If there's a riot or a hostage situation, we won't negotiate for your release." These were the last words the guard at the entrance said to us before we stored our personal belongings in lockers and prepared to go through the series of iron gates leading to the auditorium where we would minister. *Why didn't he say something before now?*

Clang! The sound of iron gates slamming shut behind me

was unnerving. I wasn't a prisoner, but for the next hour or so, I was just as trapped as they were. The song "Walk With Me," takes on new meaning when armed guards are standing a few feet away as you toot on a pitch pipe to find your note.

Singing in prison is a unique experience. Different from say, singing in church. How so? Well, let's start with the audiences. One group often listens with sullen or expressionless faces, with a spirit of heaviness radiating through hollow eyes, revealing deep longings for freedom. The other group are the prison inmates coming to worship. The intensity of their praise always blows me away. They have found something behind bars that many of their "free" brothers and sisters on the outside have yet to discover—the ability to live above their circumstances. To sing at midnight.

Two of the most famous prison singers in history were Paul and Silas. It all started with a dream Paul had of a man who was pleading with Paul to come to his town of Macedonia. Paul believed the vision to be of God and, with his companions, set out immediately for Macedonia. When they arrived in Philippi, a Roman colony and the leading city of that district of Macedonia, the missionaries went down by the Gandites River for a prayer meeting. There, they met a rich, attractive sister named Lydia. Lydia wasn't a Christian, but she worshiped God and when Paul told her about Jesus she accepted Him as her Savior.

They hadn't even reached their final destination yet and already they had their first soul. What a great way for an evangelism campaign to start!

The missionaries stayed at Lydia's bed and breakfast for a few days and began preaching and teaching in the city. It wasn't long, though, before Satan showed up to try to spoil the party.

A demon-possessed slave girl who made money for her owners as a clairvoyant, began tailing Paul and company. The first time they encountered this forerunner to "Miss Cleo," they were on their way to another prayer meeting. She started following them shouting " 'These men are servants of the Most High God, who are telling you the way to be saved' " (Acts 16:17).

Once was OK. Twice was tolerable, but after a few days, it got old. Paul couldn't hear himself think, let alone preach. He cast the demon out of the girl in the name of Jesus, and immediately the spirit left her (v. 18).

Good riddance! The miracle validates the message and the power of the missionaries and everyone is happy, right? Wrong. "Cleo's" owners suddenly lost their meal ticket and they wanted blood.

I've observed an interesting facet of human nature. People will tolerate all kinds of strange religions or bizarre philosophies, but they will be roused to violence by anything that threatens their money. Twist the Scriptures to draw a crowd? Crowds will come. Preach heresy and advocate oppressive lifestyle requirements for salvation? You'll still have supporters. But let someone fool with the money and watch out! Which only reveals the god we give the highest praise to. But I digress.

Paul and Silas were dragged "by force" into the marketplace to face the authorities, and be punished. The Jews limited such punishment to thirty-nine stripes, but Roman practice depended on the judgment of the local official—a magistrate. The magistrates had official attendants, known as lictors, each of whom carried bundles of rods as symbols of their office. These were the rods used to beat the missionaries "severely."

After their beating, they were tossed into the "inner cell" of a local prison. Roman prisons often had an outer and an inner section. In the first was the guardroom, where light and air could enter. Beyond this lay the inner prison, where, when the door was shut, light and air were excluded. Conditions in such a cell were fearful, and inflicted terrible punishment on the prisoner.

And as if this weren't enough, the men had their feet fastened in stocks. As we know them, stocks were a wooden instrument of torture with holes into which head and feet and hands were thrust, thus placing the prisoner in a most uncomfortable position. With Paul and Silas, only their feet were fastened, but this meant that their torsos were left lying on the ground. This was particularly painful because of the beating the men had taken on their backs.

Paul and Silas must have been in shock. One minute they were on assignment from God, casting out demons in Jesus' name; the next, they were in a rat-infested hellhole, with insects feeding on their oozing, bleeding wounds. Imagine how most of us would have reacted:

Silas: Can you believe this! Didn't you have a vision about coming to Macedonia and helping out?

Paul: Yes.

Silas: We came didn't we?

Paul: Yes.

Silas: Then what are we doing here? We obey the Lord and we end up beaten and in prison. What's *that* about?

Paul: I don't know.

Silas: Man, maybe that wasn't a vision. Maybe you just stayed up too late eating falafels and watching the tonight show with Jay Lenonius.

Silas: And another thing. God gave you power to cast out that demon, right? Then why didn't He give you the power to disperse that mob? If Jesus can make demons disappear, how come Jesus didn't make those rods disappear? Those rods hurt! Just look at my back! Oh, sorry, I forgot, you can't see my back because you can't *see* anything down here. There's no light! I don't get Jesus sometimes. Instead of preaching the gospel to the people we came to help, we're stuck in this hell-hole. Jesus? What's going on??? Aren't we Your children? Don't You love us anymore?

But that's not how these two men reacted. Instead of curses and complaining, Paul and Silas offered praises and petitions. From the bowels of a prison deprived of light and fresh air, came the sounds of sweet adoration.

"Praying, they were singing hymns" (v. 25), is the way the Greek expresses it. When the chips were down, when the pain was intense, when the night was dark, the missionaries did what came naturally. They worshiped. Even in a dungeon, fettered so that they could not kneel in prayer, they continued to praise their Lord.

What comes naturally to you in times of stress? Are you more likely to pray or pout? To sing or snarl? And, if you happen to fall on hard times while trying to do the right thing, what then?

Late one Friday night, I received a phone call from a trucker who lives here in the Northwest. After a sterling driving record for thirty-five years, he cracked up his rig and narrowly escaped with his life. Though the accident wasn't his fault, he lost his job and was facing the prospect of starting over at age fifty.

With tears chocking his voice, he said, "It wasn't until we started really praying that the trouble started. We began praying for our family and friends and that's when the stuff hit the fan!"

Thank God my friend wasn't ready to throw in the towel on prayer or God. But how many do when, as my late-night caller said, "the stuff hits the fan"?

Somehow, we've bought into the idea that smooth sailing equals God's smile. That clear skies indicate being in the will of God. That stormy weather and turbulence represents God's frown, and being outside of His will. Right?

Wrong! Talk about stinking thinking! Where in the Bible do you read that? This kind of thinking is the modern equivalent to Jewish thought in the time of Christ concerning sickness. Disease meant the frown of God. Remember when Jesus and His entourage came to the blind man and the disciples asked Jesus, "who sinned, this man or his parents?" (See John 9:1-3.) They made the erroneous assumption that the man's blindness was a judgment by God on his sinful life. Jesus was horrified by this kind of thinking and quickly corrected them by saying, "Neither."

Sometimes bad things happen to us as a result of poor choices we make. But sometimes bad things happen simply because we live in a world of sin. The dots don't always connect up the way we think they should.

If anything, the Bible seems to say the opposite of what we think. "In fact, everyone who wants to live a godly life in Christ Jesus will be persecuted" (2 Timothy 3:12). "Do not be surprised at the painful trial you are suffering, as though something strange were happening to you" (1 Peter 4:12). And "Consider it pure joy, my brothers, whenever you face trials of many kinds" (James 1:2).

Instead of trouble meaning you're outside of God's will, if you're living your life for Him, it could very well mean you're smack in the middle of it! Think it over. Was John the Baptist in or out of God's will when he lost his head? Was James, the brother of Jesus, in or out of God's will when he lost his? Was Stephen in or out of God's will when he was stoned? Was the apostle Paul in or out of God's will when he was given thirty-nine lashes five times from the Jews, beaten with rods three times, stoned, shipwrecked three times, and adrift at sea clinging to debris for twenty-four hours? (See 2 Corinthians 11:24, 25.)

✣

Worship attaches the fainting heart to its Savior.

Sure God delivered Daniel, and gave the Hebrew worthies asbestos suits. But He didn't deliver everyone—not even His own Son from the torture and shame of the cross. God sometimes uses trouble to bring us closer to Him—to strengthen our commitment and deepen our trust. And how we respond during times of stress can make all the difference.

Here is another great secret to help you cling to Jesus in the storms of life: Worship attaches the fainting heart to its Savior. How? How does praise and prayer help us in the time of trouble?

Surrender

First, praise leads us to an attitude of surrender. We give up our natural responses and acknowledge the sovereignty of God in their place. Notice Job's response after the most vicious storm he'd ever encountered destroyed his livestock, servants, and children.

"At this, Job got up and tore his robe and shaved his head. Then he fell to the ground in worship and said: 'Naked I came from my mother's womb, and naked I will depart. The Lord gave and the Lord has taken away; may the name of the Lord be praised' " (Job 1:20, 21).

What was that last part? Was that a typo? No, there it is. *May the name of the Lord be praised.* Job "fell to the ground in *worship.*" He surrendered to the sovereignty and will of God and maintained his connection with Him, despite his pain.

Did it hurt? Yes. Was Job's heart torn in two? You bet. Did he just "put on a happy face" and spout a pious prayer to put on a good front? No way. I can hear deep groanings and sobs behind those words, "Naked I came from my mother's womb . . ." But instead of turning from God, Job, in the depth of his grief, turned *toward* Him. He was consistent. In sunny days of prosperity and favor, Job surrendered his life to God. Now, in the day of trouble, Job does the same thing. And that is the highest form of praise.

Faith is not developed in the crisis. The crisis simply reveals the quality of the faith you already have. In an eerily prophetic sermon given just three days before the attacks on New York and Washington D.C., gospel singer and preacher Wintley Phipps asked, "Does the favor of God and a prayerful, godly life exempt the child of God from trial and persecution? No. Prayer and a godly life simply equips you to stand when the trial comes."

Crisis simply reveals the quality of the faith you already have.

Remember the words of Jesus, "In the world you *will* have tribulation." Praise reminds us that God is in control. It helps us maintain our hold on God when the storm threatens to take us under.

PRESENCE

Praise also brings the presence of God. God "inhabitest" or dwells in the praises of His people (see Psalm 22:3, KJV). And when the presence of God comes in, the presence of Satan goes out. It was Paul Billheimer who said, "Satan is allergic to praise. And wherever there is massive, triumphant praise, Satan is paralyzed, bound and banished."

Friends, anything that paralyzes, binds, and banishes the enemy is something I want to experience! And as dark as Paul and Silas's prison cell was, when they sang, the angels came to join them and the dungeon became a cathedral.

When Madame Guyon was imprisoned in the Castle of Vincennes, in 1695, she not only sang, but wrote songs of praise to her God. "It sometimes seemed to me," she said, "as if I were a little bird whom the Lord had placed in a cage, and that I had nothing now to do but to sing. The joy of my heart gave a brightness to the objects around me. The stones of my prison looked in my eyes like rubies. I esteemed them more than all the gaudy brilliancies of a vain world. My heart was full of that joy which Thou givest to them that love Thee in the midst of their greatest crosses." During one of her imprisonments, she wrote this touching little poem:

"A little bird I am,
Shut from the fields of air;
And in my songs I sit and sing
To Him who placed me there:
Well pleased a prisoner to be,
Because, my God, it pleaseth Thee."

Focus

Praise helps us to turn our eyes (also our hearts and minds) on Jesus. In the earlier fake conversation between Paul and Silas, where was the focus? On the mob, the rods, the stocks, the pain and the hurt. The only thing that could come from such a focus is what? More misery. More disappointment. More darkness, doubt, and depression. Sound familiar?

But what happened in real life was that Paul and Silas chose to focus on Jesus—to pray to Him with songs that built up their faith and gave them courage. I don't know what hymns they sang that night, but perhaps they were taken from the Psalms. Maybe the first stanza began:

The Lord is my light and my salvation;
whom shall I fear?
The Lord is the stronghold of my life;
of whom shall I be afraid? (Psalm 27:1)

A repeat followed by the second stanza . . .

My soul finds rest in God alone;
My salvation comes from him.
He alone is my rock and my salvation;
He is my fortress, I will never be shaken. (Psalm 62:1, 2)

And then the chorus . . .

Enter his gates with thanksgiving and his courts with praise;
Give thanks to him and praise his name.

For the Lord is good and his love endures forever;
His faithfulness continues through all generations. (Psalm 100:4, 5)

I don't know what they sang, but whatever it was, Tertullian's words are true:

"Though the body is shut in, though the flesh is confined, all things are open to the spirit . . . The leg does not feel the chain when the mind is in the heavens."

When my stomach is pumping acid, my mouth is dry with anxiety, and my lower back is throbbing with tension, it's because my *mind* is on something other than Jesus. Praise helps us get our minds focused on Jesus. And God promises to give perfect peace to those who keep their minds fixed on Him. (See Isaiah 26:3.)

Confidence

Praise to God eventually leads to confidence in God. I vividly recall the morning I conducted an experiment in praise. I was following Dick Eastman's outline for praying for an hour in his book, *The Hour That Changes the World*. The outline calls for the first five minutes of prayer to be spent in praise to God. No petitions, just praise. So I checked my watch, noted the time I was beginning, and then began my "experiment."

It was kind of awkward at first. I seemed to be running out of things to say all too quickly. And then something happened. Just as I was about to finish praising God for one thing, I'd suddenly remember something else. That new thought would then trigger another praiseworthy act. Then *that* act would remind me of something else wonderful about my God. And so on and so on, until it seemed I was taken over and swept away in praise. I lost track of time and awareness of the schedule I was attempting to keep. When next I checked my watch, *twenty minutes had passed by!*

And what was the result? In those twenty minutes, God grew to enormous size in my eyes. I was reminded of how good God is; how loving; how merciful; how patient; and how powerful He is. I saw that He truly was at work in my life—that He really had heard my prayers and that He had a track record with me. A track record I could depend on. And because He had worked in my life before, I could trust and have confidence that He was big enough to deal with whatever problems I was currently facing.

No one wants to join a club where the members look miserable!

Results

So what happens when we learn to sing at midnight? Let's return to the Phillippian jail.

1. The other prisoners were drawn by their witness (Acts 16:25). Singing in the shower? Nothing surprising there. But singing in

the stocks? Now that gets attention. Christian, please remember, no one wants to join a club where the members look miserable!

Oliver Wendell Holmes, Jr., was a member of the U.S. Supreme Court for thirty years. His mind, wit, and work earned him the unofficial title of "the greatest justice since John Marshall." At one point in his life, Justice Holmes explained his choice of a career by saying: "I might have entered the ministry if certain clergymen I knew had not looked and acted so much like undertakers." (Moody Bible Institute's *Today In The Word*, June, 1988, p. 13.)

Praise under pressure draws people to Christ.

2. The earth shook (v. 26). Wherever God's name is praised, angels come to join in. And at their tread, the earth trembles. Picture this scene! Still glowing from having just left the dazzling presence of the Almighty, heaven's "special forces" unit approaches the inner prison with speeds that shatter the sound barrier and shake the earth. Would to God that our prayers would cause angels to shake the earth again!

3. The captives were set free (v. 26b). "At once all the prison doors flew open, and everybody's chains came loose." Do you want out of your personal prison? Are you longing for the chains of fear and hopelessness that weigh you down to come loose? Start praising the Lord. Right now. Don't wait to feel better. Don't wait for the pain to stop hurting. Don't wait until sunrise. Right now, in the dark. Begin to sing. Praise the Lord. Worship. And

wait. God is about to "rock your world" and you're going free.

There once was a conference at a Presbyterian church in Omaha. People were given helium-filled balloons and told to release them at some point in the service when they felt like expressing the joy in their hearts. Being of conservative mindset, they didn't feel free to say "Hallelujah! Praise the Lord!" So they let the balloons do their talking for them. All through the service balloons ascended, but when it was over one third of the balloons were unreleased.

Let your balloon go.

❖

Lord, I'll be the first to admit that my first reaction to problems is not praise. My first reaction is to lash out in anger or to try to fix whatever is wrong. If I can't fix it, I'll often blame You. Forgive me, Lord, and teach me to sing at midnight—to trust You in the dark as well as in the light. Show me how to focus on You instead of on my problems. Help my life to be a continual act of worship so that I may experience Your presence at all times and in all circumstances. Transform my "prisons" into cathedrals, and send angels of strength and comfort to my side, the way You sent angels to Paul and Silas. Release me from fear and from whatever is holding me back from completely trusting Your plan for my life. Amen.

"Call upon Me in the day of trouble;

I will deliver you,

and you shall glorify Me."

" 'And everyone who calls on

the name of the Lord

will be saved.' "

—Psalm 50:15; Acts 2:21

4

Let not your heart be troubled . . .

About Death

Have you ever lost a day's worth of work because of a power surge or some other computer glitch? If you don't work with computers, you can't relate. But those of you who do know the agony I'm talking about. Just yesterday my daughter Crystal dissolved into tears because the program she wrote to create a Web page—a program she had worked on until the wee hours of the morning for several days in a row—somehow got corrupted. This school project was due for grading, and after all her hours of work, she stuck the disk in the computer at school and got only an error message. For most of the day, Crystal was inconsolable. She had nothing to show for all her late nights and hard work. It was inexplicably, irretrievably, and sadly gone.

Computers can be cruel. So can life. One second the quarterly report, book chapter, or Web page program we've spent hours and hours to create is there on the screen; the next it's gone. One second the relationships we've spent a lifetime establishing are ours to enjoy, the next, they're gone in the twisted metal of a car wreck, or in the smoldering rubble of a collapsed skyscraper. We can't explain why computer programs get corrupted and our work evaporates into cyberspace anymore than we can explain why bodies get diseased and our loved ones are taken away from us in death. But we still want answers, don't we?

The search for answers

"We search for the truth," the sign read. "We seek Justice. The courts require it. The victims cry for it. And God demands it!" These words were spray-painted in tall, black letters on April 19, 1995, by a firefighter from Team 5 on a brick wall across the street from the Alfred P. Murrah Federal building in Oklahoma City. At 9:00 that fateful morning, hundreds of federal employees were at their desks going about their daily tasks. At 9:02, a truck bomb detonated and blew away a third of the building along with 168 lives. There one minute. Gone the next.

An unidentified firefighter expressed his outrage in graffiti and demanded justice. And as I snapped photos of the 168 empty chairs facing a reflecting pool at the heart of the memorial site—each chair representing a life lost in the blast—I wanted justice too. And, like so many others, I asked the *Why* questions.

The *Why* questions are asked in every hospital and nursing home. They are asked at the scene of tragic accidents. They are asked in bug-infested inner city apartments where children go to sleep hungry every night on filthy, threadbare mattresses, to the sounds of curses and gunfire as their lullaby. They are asked on battlefields, refugee camps, and in the bullet-riddled hallways of upper-middle-class, suburban high schools. The questions are asked in cemeteries, at crisis centers, in Barrios, and most recently in New York City, Washington, D.C., and in rural Pennsylvania.

And as we ask *Why,* two-thirds of the world's population wonders why we're just now asking. For the majority of people who call planet Earth home, the United States is the Johnny-come-lately to the pity party. How many billions exist in conditions that we wouldn't even submit our pets to? Places where terror and hunger and loss are as common to everyday life as McDonald's, cable, and cell phones are to everyday life here in America.

We ask the questions now because the pain is touching us. And frankly, that's when we all ask the questions—when hurt comes to our neighborhood; when suffering looks up our address; when loss is our unwelcome houseguest.

And what of the answers? Are there any?

The virus of sin

Even as viruses destroy computer files, and anthrax poisons the body, sin destroys whatever it touches. All disease, misery, and death are mere symptoms of this root dysfunction. Sin—rebellion against the law, character, and government of God—results in death to all who are infected (see Romans 6:23), and, unfortunately, the entire human race has been exposed (see Romans 3:23).

Even as viruses destroy computer files, and Anthrax poisons the body, sin destroys whatever it touches.

Because of our sin-sickness, our lives are "a mist that appears for a little while and then vanishes" (James 4:14). Whether we live to be ninety-five, like my grandmother Pearl, or five, like many of the children who perished in the Murrah building's daycare center, life is tragically short. The days of vibrant health, and boundless energy without stiff joints, dimming sight, fading memory, portable teeth, swollen prostates, lumpy breasts, thinning hair, and leaky hearts are few.

And while we're all marching toward our date with death,

what's God doing about it? As we suffer the insidious decay of sin and suffer the injustices of life, what does Jesus do?

JESUS WEEPS . . . AND SAVES

Across the street from the Oklahoma memorial site is a statue of a weeping Jesus. Clutching his robe with one hand and holding his face in the other, the grief-stricken Jesus has his back turned to the memorial and faces a wall that has 168 missing bricks. Again, each missing brick represents a life lost in the explosion. The statue depicts Christ's disapproval of the atrocity, and his heartache for the victims. A small plaque on the statue's base reads, "Jesus Wept."

Jesus sympathizes with the human condition because He knows what it's like to be human. He is not "a high priest who is unable to sympathize with our weaknesses," (see Hebrews 4:15). No, Jesus cares about what happens to us. He rejoices when we rejoice, and weeps when we weep.

But if that's all He did, it wouldn't be enough, would it? If that were the extent of God's involvement in our sorrow, what good would that do? There are enough tears being shed on planet Earth to go around. I can get sympathy from my doctor, or my spouse, or my friends. If I want someone to cry with when my heart breaks, I'll find somebody. But I need more from Jesus. And thank God, He does do more than cry. He saves.

When Jesus saw Mary and her friends weeping over Lazarus's death, "he was deeply moved in spirit and troubled" (John 11:33). The compassionate Jesus felt loss—not only the loss of one man who was His friend, but the loss the entire human family must endure while confined to this planet. Knowing that we have to feel the sting of death as long as we live broke His heart. So "Jesus wept" (v. 35).

Some who watched the tears fall from Jesus' eyes were moved by the depth of feeling Jesus displayed. But others wanted to know why He didn't do more. " 'Could not he who opened the eyes of the blind man have kept this man from dying?' " (v. 37.) They had seen the other miracles and wondered why He didn't work a miracle for His friend.

We wonder too, don't we? Where was the miracle-working Jesus when my child was dying with cancer? Where was His power when my loved one needed a kidney? What was God doing when Timothy McVeigh parked his death truck in front of the Murrah building, or when the terrorists hijacked those airliners? Jesus was a miracle-worker, true enough. But He was so much more.

A MIRACLE THAT LASTS

The healings of flaccid limbs, opaque eyes, and leperous flesh, were representative of the real healing Jesus came to provide.

Those miracles weren't intended to be ends in and of themselves. They were Jesus' means of drawing people to Himself so that they would believe that He was who He said He was—the Messiah, the Deliverer, the Savior. Jesus provided a temporary blessing to encourage belief in His permanent solution.

Jesus provided a temporary blessing to encourage belief in His permanent solution.

That's right. The healings of Jesus were *temporary*. Everyone who was healed by Jesus eventually got some other disease or grew old and died! Jairus's daughter that Jesus raised from the dead? She grew up, got old, and died. The woman with the bleeding problem who touched the hem of Jesus' garment and was made instantly well? *Died.* The paralytic who had laid by the pool of Bethesda for thirty-eight years before Jesus healed him? *Died.* Jesus knew that everyone He touched was still subject to sin and its death sentence. This mortal life that we know on planet Earth is marked by a cycle of birth, growth, and death. And even if death is suspended temporarily by modern medicine or a divine miracle of intervention, eventually, the sin virus claims all. That is why none of the people whom Jesus cured are walking around today!

THE MIRACLE OF GRACE

But the good news is that while not everyone gets the temporary type of miracle described above, every man, woman, boy and girl can possess the greater miracle of God's grace which cures sin and provides permanent, everlasting life.

" 'Which is easier,' " Jesus said to the skeptical religious leaders of his day, " 'to say, "Your sins are forgiven you," or to say, "Get up and walk"?' " (Luke 5:23). If we're not careful, in our haste to find temporary relief from our pain, we might say, "anybody can talk about sin and all that spiritual jazz, but it takes a lot of power to make someone walk!"

To provide a temporary miracle of healing took just a word, to provide the permanent miracle of grace to forgive the sins of humanity took His life.

But Jesus was one with God, remember? He was, in fact, the Creator of everything that is. "Through him all things were made; without him nothing was made that has been made. In him was life, and that life was the light of men" (John 1:3, 4). It was not a hard thing for the Life-Giver to say "Get up and walk." He who spoke worlds into being could surely speak pulsating energy and life into palsied limbs. But as wonderful as this might be, this power to heal physically was secondary and inferior to the power it took for Him to say "Your sins are forgiven." Why? Because *to provide a temporary miracle of healing took just a word, to provide the permanent miracle of grace to forgive the sins of humanity took His life.* The antidote and ultimate cure for every hurt, disease, and pain of humanity, is the precious blood of Jesus Christ that had to be spilled in order for humans to be saved by it.

This is the mightiest and most mind-boggling miracle of all—that the sinless Christ, "who knew no sin," was made sin for us "that we might be the righteousness of God" (2 Corinthians 5:21,NKJV). And this miracle—the miracle of grace—is *free* to everyone who calls on the name of Jesus. This is the miracle Jesus came to give us. That's a Jesus who does more than cry. That's a God I can cry out to in my distress, because I know He can do something about it.

Jesus wept. And that means we can weep too. If God feels pain, who are we to think we can't grieve? Christians die and bury their dead just like non-Christians do. We hurt just like everyone else hurts. Jesus never said not to grieve over death. Death is still our enemy. He just told us not to fear it, and not to grieve as those who have no hope (see 1 Thessalonians 4:13). Why? Because His death on the cross makes our death on this earth *temporary*.

Death for the Christian is like when a computer goes down in a lightning storm. The screen goes temporarily dark. The data that was there is temporarily off the scene and unusable. If your file wasn't saved, it's gone for good—evaporated into cyberspace. You, like my daughter Crystal, have reason to weep, wail, and gnash your teeth.

But! If your data has been saved, it may be off the screen at the moment, but nothing's been lost. All you have to do is *reboot*. While the computer is rebooting, you get a lot of junk at first, but once the program is active, you hit "File," "Open" and your document is back.

When I delivered my grandmother's eulogy, I made this analogy. "Mama" knew Jesus. She had accepted His grace in place of her sins. Jesus *saved* her. Because Mama was *saved* nothing of her was lost. After ninety-five years (666 weeks, 34,000 days, 832,200 hours, 49,932,000 minutes) she's off the screen for the moment, but Jesus is simply rebooting the program. Ever since sin knocked humanity off line, God has been doing more than weeping over His lost children. He's working to reboot our program. During the process, we contend with a lot of junk—trials and tribulations—but soon Jesus will open up the sky and execute the restore command and say, "Arise, ye that sleep in the dust and awake." He will say to the north, " ' "Give them up!" and to the south, "Do not hold them back" (Isaiah 43:6). And Mama will come forth not as she went down when the power failed, but better than ever in the full bloom of youth, and shoutin' hallelujah!

And so will Mary, my mother-in-law.

And so will Grandma Reva, and Grandpa L.V.

And so will cousin Bobby.

And so will my neighbor, Bob.

And so will Andrew.

And so will that priest who died administering last rites to one of the victims in the World Trade Center.

And so will that infant child who was killed in the car wreck that occurred while his parents were on their way to attend a prayer seminar I was conducting in Lewiston, Idaho.

And so will the multiplied millions of believers who clung to Jesus during their lifetimes and called on His name. They are off the screen of daily life for now. But they are not lost. Unlike my daughter's homework assignment, they were "saved." We'll see them again.

Don't let your heart be troubled Mr. Firefighter from Team 5. Justice will come for the victims of Oklahoma City. It will come for the victims of Washington, D.C., New York City, Afghanistan, and for the victims of sin in every age, everywhere on planet Earth. The God who weeps *and* saves will wipe every tear from our eyes and make all things new. (See Revelation 21:4, 5.) Permanently.

❖

Thank You, Lord, for being more than a God who weeps. Thank You for Your tears and for what You sacrificed to remove ours. Because Your Son was willing to go to the cross in our place and leave You forever, we can walk through the valley of the shadow of death with You and fear no evil. Our lives are safe in Your hands. Help us to choose You today and forever. Amen.

This is what the Lord says—he who created you …

"Fear not, for I have redeemed you;

I have summoned you by name;

you are mine."

—Isaiah 43:1

5

Let not your heart be troubled . . .

About God's Love for You

I love weddings. Especially weddings as visually and spiritually beautiful as the one I attended last weekend. The bride is the oldest daughter of a good friend, fellow church member, and colleague of mine. We've known Tina for nearly fifteen years and she's been a real friend of the family. Scott, the groom, is fairly new to our church, joining by baptism only a year ago. He and Tina locked eyes and, later, hearts in our church choir, and almost immediately began making beautiful music together.

Last Sunday, their love for each other brought them to the

altar to become husband and wife. The guests who attended will remember many things from this wedding: how good our vintage '70s church interior looked despite the orange pews, gold carpet, and dark wood paneling; how the choir sounded as they sang "Surely the Presence of the Lord is in This Place," while standing along the walls of the dimly lit sanctuary, holding lighted long-tapered candles. They'll remember Tina's expression of pure joy as she walked down the aisle and curtsied to her proud father who bowed to her before handing her over to his future son-in-law.

But the apex of the nuptials, and the moment that will linger longest on the film of our memories occurred when Scott read a poem of his own creation to his bride and best friend. Having just been pronounced husband and wife by our pastor, he turned to face the woman he had just promised to love for the rest of his life, and said:

Tina, you're the answer to my prayer.
With you and God I see a better life.
Tina, I want you to know each time I pray,
I'll thank the Lord that you're my wife.
My promise now to you, my love,
there is one thing I will do.
I will love you the way that God says that I should,
And always be there for you.

Take this to heart and remember, because, for you, I'll always care
Come what may, I'll always know
You're the answer to my prayer.

—Scott Sanders, © 2001. (Used by permission.)

The hankies were in full bloom, wiping and dabbing at moist eyes all over the building. But the floodgates really let loose when Scott ended his poem by singing "You Are So Beautiful to Me." The sincerity and passion with which he sang the line: "You're everything that I've hoped for; you're everything to me," held his beloved, and the rest of us, spellbound. It was a sacred moment of declared love. No one left that sanctuary with any doubts about how Tina and Scott felt about each other. (Not after *that* kiss!) There was no questioning of their status. They walked down that gold-carpeted center aisle (mercifully covered by the white runner), as husband and wife. Two hearts had become one. They belonged to God and to each other.

An inconceivable thought to anyone who knows this couple would be that either would fear the other. That come Monday morning, or three days into the honeymoon, the radiant bride would succumb to feelings of anxiety and depression caused by fears that Scott really didn't love her after all. That the poem was a pretense. The kiss was a sham. That not only didn't he love her, but Scott was actually trying to dissolve the marriage and kick her out of his life.

And though anyone who has observed this couple over the past year would dismiss as crazy this notion I just described, how many Christians torment themselves with the fear that God doesn't really love them? That despite the promises of forgiveness and invitations of grace, God is actually trying to dissolve our marriage to Him and is trying to kick us out of His kingdom? Sad to say, it's more than you imagine.

Afraid of God

Recently, my mother had a phone conversation with one of her sisters. The talk turned to terrorism and how it was affecting our lives. Mom was affirming how good it was to know that God is ultimately in control no matter what, when my aunt made an astonishing admission. A long-time Christian, history buff, and student of Bible prophecy, my aunt confessed that, in truth, she was just as scared of God as she was of what was happening in our world. When Mother asked her why, she responded, "When I think of God and who He is; a God able to create a world and everything in it, and keep it going—a God so awesome and holy—and then I look at myself and how sinful and puny I am—well, I can't see myself standing before Him without being consumed."

She was afraid of the terrorists and she was afraid of God. Panicked by evil on one hand, and panicked by holiness on the other. And if this were an isolated case, we could shrug it off as a fluke and keep marching to Zion. But my aunt is not alone in feeling this way.

The truth is, generations of Bible-believing, tithe-paying, clean-living, and church-attending Christians grew up with the notion that God was really trying to keep us *out* of heaven, and that no matter how good we tried to be, He was going to expose us for the frauds we are and nail us in the judgment.

Don't believe me? Another relative recently called my mother in a near state of panic after hearing a statement from a local elder. Apparently, this man told the Bible study class that no one knows when his or her name comes up for review before God. That once God reviews a particular case, that person's "probation" closes and their fate, as far as eternity is concerned, is sealed. This means, according to this elder, that there are a lot of "dead men walking" in the world, and even in the church today. People who, while they were "in a far country" spiritually, and not living for God, have had their probation closed by God who had judged them and found them outside of His will. It didn't matter, said the elder, if they subsequently repented of their sins, returned to "the fold" and started living for God. For them it was too little, too late. They may be in the church every time the door opens now, but it's meaningless in the scheme of things. Case closed.

The elder may as well have had a loaded pistol. It wouldn't have frightened my cousin any worse than the words he had just heard. Why? Because he had, in fact, only recently returned to the Lord after a time of straying. The last few years had been especially sweet as he and his wife renewed their love affair with the God they had been raised to believe would save them to the uttermost. Never had God seemed so close. Never had His fellowship been as sweet. They were sacrificing to put their children in a Christian school, growing in their prayer and devotional lives, and enjoying the rekindled romance of their first-love experience with Christ.

The storms of life are intimidating enough without being afraid that the Captain of our rescue ship is trying to drown us!

But sitting in church that day, my cousin was stricken by the thought that maybe it was all a lie. That perhaps God had already judged him during his earlier rebellious per-iod, and that he was now a "dead man" in heaven's eyes. Maybe he only thought he was in a saving relationship with Jesus, when in fact divorce proceedings had already taken place.

I must tell you that I got angry when I heard about this. Angry because my friend didn't hear this distortion of God's character from a Bible-hating atheist. No, he got it from a church leader in the pew of his own local church! The lie came from *inside* the family of God, which only goes to show how little some of us know Him. The storms of life are intimidating enough without being afraid that the Captain of our rescue ship is trying to drown us!

Crazy about Us

Please believe this if you don't believe anything else: *God is not trying to keep us out of heaven.* To the contrary. He's done and is doing everything in His infinite power, including going to hell and back, to get us in! If God wanted to do away with sinners, He didn't need to become a man, live in poverty, and die on a cross to do it. Why go to all that trouble if He wanted to disown us and cut us out of His "will"?

You don't die for someone, then turn your back on them. You don't give blood to save somebody and then slit their throats. That's the good news of the gospel—that God loves us and is for us. (See Romans 8:31.) I'll be the first to confess that I don't understand how He could love me, but I'm so glad He does! God doesn't possess love as a character trait like you and I do. He doesn't *have* love, He *is* love. He is the embodiment of what love is. Therefore, it is His nature to love. He can't help Himself. It's who He is. And He's crazy about us. Crazy enough to ransom His throne in order to bring us home safely.

But it is our inability and reluctance to receive His free gift of salvation that keeps us hostage to fear of the judgment and robs us of any joy. Consider the two fears the individuals above have towards God.

Fear of God's Holiness

People have been afraid of God ever since Adam and Eve were caught hiding from Him in the bushes. Sin does that. It separates us from God, who is holy and is "a consuming fire." (Hebrews 12:29).

When God spoke the law to Moses in the hearing of His newly liberated people at the base of Mount Sinai, the Hebrews quaked in fear (see Exodus 20:18-21). When Isaiah saw the Lord "high and exalted" in the temple, where six-winged seraphs called to each other " 'Holy, holy, holy is the Lord Almighty; the whole earth is full of his glory,' " (Isaiah 6:1-3), the prophet was overcome with an awareness of his sinfulness. He had seen the King, and in contrast to His holiness, Isaiah felt ruined and utterly base.

The realization of our smallness in the eyes of God is where reverence begins.

Was this a wrong reaction? Absolutely not. It's the *only* reaction sinners can have in the presence of a holy and awesome God. The realization of our smallness in the eyes of God is where reverence begins—something sadly lacking in most modern forms of worship today. (I still remember the Christian concert I attended at a large church in my neighborhood where the young people took turns hitting beach balls to each other in the sanctuary while waiting for the concert to begin! Call me old-fashioned, but I don't think playing beach volleyball in the sanctuary remotely qualifies as "reverence"!)

But God's people aren't to live in fear of Him. Read the rest of Isaiah's encounter with God. The very thing that made the prophet cower and quake in the presence of the Almighty—his own wretchedness—was taken care of. "Then one of the seraphs flew to me with a live coal in his hand, which he had taken with tongs from the altar. With it he touched my mouth and said, 'See, this has touched your lips; your guilt is *taken away and your sin atoned for*' " (Isaiah 6:6, emphasis supplied).

My aunt said that she couldn't see standing before such an awesome God in her sinfulness. And I say, Auntie, you were never intended to stand before Him in your sinfulness! That's why Jesus stands *for us* in His righteousness.

There we are, like Joshua the high priest, standing before the angel of the Lord with Satan playing the role of prosecutor, accusing him of his sin. (See Zechariah 3:1-5.) He can't deny the things Satan is saying. They're all true! The lying, the cheating, the bad attitude, the foul mouth, the quick temper, the racial slurs, the stolen tithe, the lustful thoughts, the selfish ambition—it's all true! For him and for us, it's all true.

But praise the Lord, He doesn't see our rags. He sees the clean clothes of His Son's righteousness covering our nakedness. I like the way Janet Congo expresses it in her poem, "It's A Process."

Yes, it is true that when you stand before the Lord to ask His forgiveness,
Your dress is ragged and tattered because of ugly sins,
Your hair is thickly tangled with the web of rebellion,
Your shoes are torn and muddy by your past failures.
But God never sees any of that!
He sees you holy,
He sees you perfect
Because you are dressed in His righteousness
And He has covered you with the full length cape of His love.
He sees nothing else!
Even when you explain how you really look underneath,
He hears but He forgets forever.
The dimension of His forgiveness is as far as the East is from the West,
And it endures past all eternity.

This is the good news of the gospel. That we whose attempts at do-gooding are as "filthy rags," whose "whole head is sick, and the whole heart faints" (Isaiah 1:5), and who are "ruined" in His presence, have had our guilt "taken away" by Jesus Christ. Our sins are "atoned for."

That's why Christians don't need to be in terror of God's holiness. Respect it, yes. Be in awe of Him, yes. But quake with fear of Him? Only if you don't have a relationship with Him.

Relationship Makes the Difference

Though the photo was first published in the early 1960s, the black and white image of "John-John" at play under President Kennedy's desk in the oval office remains a treasured and enduring symbol of our nation's youth and innocence. There, in the seat of ultimate human power—the desk of the president of the United States—John F. Kennedy, Jr. is peeking out playfully from an open panel in the desk, while the president attends to business in the background.

What business the president is involved in we don't know. But whatever the most powerful man on earth was doing, the little boy isn't being told to leave. No CIA or sunglass-wearing secret service agents are dragging the toddler away. Why? *Because of the relationship the boy has with the president.* J.F.K., Jr. is at ease and welcome in the president's presence because the president is his dad.

The fourth chapter of the book of Revelation describes the

ultimate seat of power in the universe—the throne of God. It is an awesome scene of majesty and mind-boggling power, where, from a rainbow-encircled throne comes "flashes of lightnings, rumblings and peals of thunder" (Revelation 4:5). Around the throne are four living creatures and twenty-four elders who continually offer praise and give glory to the Almighty God who sits on that throne. A place of holiness and awe? No question. A place for sinful human beings like you and me? *You bet!*

When we pray, we enter, by faith, the throne room of heaven. And just like John-John in the oval office, no angelic guard—no Cherubim or Seraphim—bars our admittance. Why? *Because of our relationship to the King!* That's our "Dad" sitting on that throne!

It's all about relationship. If I attempt to stand before a holy God in my sinful nakedness, I'm toast. But If I've accepted Jesus as my personal Lord and Savior, I'm a member of God's household (see Ephesians 2:19), and have nothing to fear.

Fear of God's Judgment

I've seen paintings of Jesus standing by the side of a fearful human being acting as his Mediator in the awesome courtroom of heaven. In the painting Jesus is making a defense for the sinner to the Judge on the bench. Presumably, God the Father is sitting on the bench enshrouded by light, hearing the case. But if those paintings were to be accurate, Jesus would occupy both positions. That's right! Jesus is both Defense Attorney and Judge in the courtroom of heaven. Hear His own words:

" 'Moreover, the Father judges no one, but has entrusted all judgment to the Son, that all may honor the Son just as they honor the Father' " (John 5:22, 23).

That means you and I have a friend in court! Judgment Day for the believer is not a day to fear, but rather a day to rejoice! Judgment is not condemnation day, it is vindication day—the day Jesus rejects Satan's claims on my life, and takes the filthy garments of sin from me forever. (See Zechariah 3:1-5.)

Some people make a life's study of the beasts, prophetic time lines, and mystical symbols of Daniel and Revelation. Nothing wrong with that. But if your study of these books leads to terror and despair, you've missed the point.

If you know nothing about the judgment except one thing, know this: *the judgment is in favor of the saints!* Mark it in your Bibles right now. Daniel 7:22: " '. . . the Ancient of Days came and pronounced judgment *in favor of the saints* of the Most High, and the time came when they possessed the kingdom' " (emphasis supplied).

Did you see that? Judgment is "in favor of the saints." And who are "the saints of the Most High"? ". . . those who are sanctified in Christ Jesus, called to be saints" (1 Corinthians 1:2).

Throughout the New Testament, "saints" are defined as followers of the Lord, Jesus Christ. If that describes you, then you are "fellowcitizens with *the saints,* and of the household of God" (Ephesians 2:19, KJV, emphasis supplied). You are among those whom God gives a favorable judgment, and are entitled to possess the kingdom!

✤

Judgment Day for the believer is not a day to fear, but rather a day to rejoice!

Hallelujah! The "Ancient of Days" comes to court, not to condemn the saints, but to "pronounce judgment in [our] favor"! For believers in Jesus, there is no need to fear the judgment. We should celebrate it and look forward to it.

Receiving the gift

However, you can't celebrate what you've never claimed as your own. Salvation is the free gift of God, but it's still something we struggle to accept. Why is this so? Some traditions teach that only God knows ultimately who will or won't be saved. Consequently, declaring that one is "saved" is presumptuous and shouldn't be done.

While I agree that God alone knows who are truly His, I believe strongly that we must declare our status with God if we're to possess the assurance of our salvation. The Bible says "That if you confess with your mouth, 'Jesus is Lord,' and believe in your heart that God raised him from the dead, you will be saved. For it is with your heart that you believe and are justified, and *it is with your mouth that you confess and are saved*" (Romans 10:9, 10, emphasis supplied). Many Christians have "believed in their hearts"—they've mentally accepted the fact that Jesus is Lord and that God raised Him from the dead. But they've resisted the part about confessing with the mouth. This is crucial to our ability to receive the gift we've been given because "it is with your mouth that you confess and are saved."

You can't celebrate what you've never claimed as your own.

It's like a marriage. At Scott and Tina's wedding, the couple stood before God, family and friends and openly declared their love for one another. They entered into a covenant relationship and declared their new status.

But what if they had never declared their vows and just "lived together"? Tina would never know where Scott really stood with her. There would be nothing binding between them, and there would always be a sense of insecurity and uncertainty in their relationship. Many Christians are just trying their best to "live with" God. Trying to please Him. Trying to do what they believe is required of them, but never enjoying the rest and security of a covenant relationship with Him.

Like marriage, baptism is a public declaration of our decision to follow Jesus. We stand before God, family and friends and openly declare our love for God and our decision to make Him the Lord of our lives. Those who choose daily to live as His child need not live in fear or ambiguity about their status with God.

"God has given us eternal life," says John, "and this life is in His Son [not in my goodness, of which I have none]. He who has the Son has life, he who does not have the Son of God does not have life. I write these things to you who believe in the name of the Son of God, so that you may *know* that you have eternal life" (1 John 5:11-13, emphasis supplied).

No guessing. No wondering. No hoping and no wishing. Those who "have the Son" are to *know* that they have eternal life. If Jesus is yours, He has saved you. And it's time for the Redeemed of the Lord to say so! (See Psalm. 107:2.)

" 'I tell you the truth,' " Jesus said, " 'whoever hears my word and believes him who sent me *has eternal life* and will *not be condemned;* he has crossed over [past tense; it's already happened] from death to life' " (John 5:24; emphasis supplied).

Don't misunderstand. I do not support the popular teaching of "once saved, always saved." God respects our freedom of choice above all else. He won't force us to stay with Him. Jesus said that no man would be able to pluck us from His Father's hand (see John 10:29). This is absolutely true. We can, of our own free will, however, choose to jump out of it. (See 2 Peter 2:20-22.) But why would we ever leave the Lover of our souls? The One who has done so much for us?

Receive the gift of salvation. Embrace it with your heart and with your mouth. Declare this day that "I am my beloved's and my beloved is mine"! (Song of Solomon 6:3) Hear His words of betrothal and love to you today:

"I have loved you with an everlasting love;
I have drawn you with loving-kindness (Jeremiah 31:3).
"I am the Lord, your God,
the Holy One of Israel, your Savior;
I give Egypt for your ransom,
Cush and Seba in your stead.
Since you are precious and honored in my sight,
and because I love you,
I will give men in exchange for you,
and people in exchange for your life.
Do not be afraid, for I am with you" . . . (Isaiah 43:3-5, emphasis supplied).

THE WEDDING

The day is coming when you will stand before your Lord, not in fear and trembling, but as a bride adorned for her husband. And though I know it's hard for you to believe it right now, the One who has given so much to make sure you spend eternity by His side " 'will take great delight in you, he will quiet you with his love, he will rejoice over you with singing' " (Zephaniah 3:17).

And what will He sing? "You are so beautiful to me. You're everything I hoped for, you're everything to me. You are so beautiful, to me."

❖

Lord, I can't believe You love me this much! I am nothing, and You are everything. Help me to stop being afraid of You and to receive the gift of salvation that You paid for with Your life. I believe in my heart, now I want to confess with my mouth—You are my Lord; thank You for saving me! Cover my wretchedness, Jesus, and hide me in Your holiness. You are so beautiful to me! Amen.

"Do not let your hearts be troubled.
Trust in God; trust also in me.
In my Father's house are many rooms;
if it were not so, I would have told you.
I am going there to prepare a place for you.
And if I go and prepare a place for you,
I will come back and take you to be with me."

—John 14:1-3

6

Let not your heart be troubled . . .

About the End

We were in a large, communal cell, with scarcely any room to walk, let alone to sit or lie down. Our captors were drunk with the power they held over us.

How quickly things had changed! Only weeks ago, we had been law-abiding citizens, protected by the Constitution. Then, if we had encountered one of these prison guards on the street, or in the mall, we would have smiled at each other. No more. Now sneers replaced smiles. Curses supplanted courtesies. Brutality smothered brotherhood.

Overnight we had become the enemy. Breathing was a chore in that stagnant space. Like Salmon "climbing the ladder" to spawn in an Alaskan hatchery, we were jammed together too tightly to do much of anything—but pray. And pray we did—for deliverance, for strength, for peace of mind since peace of body was impossible.

Suddenly, the ground began to shake. It started as a low, almost imperceptible rumble. The faces of our tormentors that had been twisted in sadistic glee, became instantly dark and sober. Even as the shaking intensified, they gave a knowing look of acceptance and moved roboticly to the cell doors and unlocked them. In amazement we watched as they flung the doors open wide and gestured for us to make our escape.

Somehow we knew.

So did they.

It was over.

Our flight to freedom was exhilarating and improbable. The earthquake was at its peak of violence causing the surrounding hills and valleys to heave and swell like waves on the ocean, while the earth beneath our feet remained solid. Everywhere we looked we witnessed indescribable chaos and mayhem. Yet we felt perfectly calm. Like standing in the eye of a hurricane.

How many were with us as we ran, I couldn't say. But our feet kept moving us forward and eventually carried us to a seashore. By now a multitude had gathered on the sand. A rainbow of humanity stretched before me as far as my eyes could see. Black, White, Asian, Hispanic, Arab—all colors, cultures, and people groups were represented. There, to my left were Catholic nuns in their habits. To my right, a Native American in full tribal dress. None of those differences mattered now. There was only one group. Believers. And we were together for the same reason. We were waiting for our ride home.

The horizon disappeared as gray surf merged with an overcast sky that sagged like a vagrant's tired overcoat. Suddenly, a young woman bolted to the water's edge and pointed at something in the mist above.

"Look!" She shouted.

Like the map of Nevada that burns from the inside out at the beginning of the old *Bonanza* TV show, the clouds appeared to ignite and burn back from a central point in space, revealing a scene of unspeakable glory. Supported on a column of cloud was a golden throne framed on either side by serpentine staircases that disappeared into a dazzling building. Seated on the throne was Christ Himself, so high and awash in glory that His features were impossible to see.

For a moment, all was silent. The convulsing of the elements ceased and every mouth was hushed. Then, from behind the throne came a sound. It started like a whisper, and soon swelled to a deafening roar. What was it? Cheering? Yes! Like the thunderous noise of 60,000 screaming fans at Yankee stadium, a roar of cheering came cascading from the twin staircases that were suddenly filled with angels. Running. Running and cheering at the top of their lungs! Multiplied millions of angelic beings ran with ridiculous speed down the stairs and off the clouds toward us.

✤

In an instant we were engulfed in arms as strong as steel, held fast by love as vast as eternity.

In an instant we were engulfed in arms as strong as steel, held fast by love as vast as eternity. We were laughing and crying at the same time.

"We're so glad you made it!" the angels gushed through tear-streaked cheeks—their beautiful faces radiant with joy. "We were pulling for you, praying that you wouldn't give up! Praise God, you made it!"

It is impossible to describe our joy. We were seeing, and touching, our guardian angels for the first time. Those celestial body guards and companions who kept us out of harm's way and out of Satan's snare from the cradle to this moment on the sand, were now revealed.

The wildest family reunions you could imagine were taking place all around us. Husbands reunited with wives, mothers reunited with sons, dads and granddads reunited with their families. Death had lost its power to separate. Loved ones who had been sleeping in their graves heard the voice of their Savior calling them by name, and they left their dusty beds to join the party! In the words of Dr. Martin Luther King, Jr., "Free at last! Free at last! Thank God Almighty, we're free at last!"

FINAL LEG OF THE JOURNEY

That dream of long ago left a lasting impression on me. I'm sure it's been at least twenty years since I dreamed it. I remember writing it down because it affected me so deeply. But I can't find it now. I searched my files, but came up empty. After twenty years anything could have happened to a piece of paper where I scribbled down a dream. (Especially if you've seen my, er, "filing system.")

No matter. It's imbedded in my mind and heart forever. And even though it was just a dream, it reminds me of the day we'll leave Planet Trouble behind and go home to the Kingdom of Love.

There I go talking about home again. Sorry, I can't help it. Whenever I travel (and I do my share), I get most excited on the final leg of the journey—when I'm closest to home. When the pilot turns on the seat belt sign for the last time as we begin our descent, and the flight attendants are making their final safety checks in preparation for landing, my heart begins to beat just a little faster. I'm not thinking of getting up at 4:00 in the morning so I could make the 90 minute drive to the airport, return the rental car and check in an hour and half before departure time. I'm not thinking of the bad airline food, the screaming kid who sat next to me half way across the country, or the roller coaster turbulence we encountered along the way.

✣

The hassles of the journey fade into insignificance when I get close to home.

The hassles of the journey fade into insignificance when I get close to home. I'm going to see my Honey. I'm going to get humongous hugs from my kids. I'm going to sleep in my own bed and eat some much-missed home cooking. I'm even anxious to see the dog.

Home! Is there anything like going home?

I captured a homegoing moment on video back in the Spring of 2000. My wife and I were returning from a ministry trip to St. Croix, Virgin Islands. We had had a wonderful time of fellowship there. Friendly people, exquisite singing, tropical breezes, Tamarind juice and coconut water (OK, the coconut water is an acquired taste!), azure-colored water and white sand beaches are just a few of the pleasures we enjoyed there.

By the time we reached Chicago's O'Hare airport, we were

exhausted. The trip had been long. First a puddle jumper from St. Croix to Puerto Rico. Then a connection from Puerto Rico to Chicago. And finally, the last leg that would take us from Chicago home to Boise. As we got on the moving walkway that runs underground between terminal B and C at O'Hare, I whipped out the video camera and interviewed Suzette about the trip and about finally going home.

"Are you tired?" you can hear me asking. She nods her head yes to the tune of "Rhapsody in Blue" playing over the PA system.

"Ready to see the girls?"

Again she nods her head affirmatively while gazing at the neon lights dancing above our heads.

The underground walkway at O'Hare is pretty cool. But we weren't about to move in. It's an architecturally-fascinating tunnel, but it is a tunnel. There's no evidence on the video that we set down our bags and started measuring for curtains. Nope. The bags were still hanging from our shoulders. We were still clutching our tickets. This was not a stopping place. We were simply passing through.

The video continues. Suzette now turns to face the camera. She says something, but it's lost in the din of that tunnel. You can't hear her, but you can read her lips very clearly. "I'm ready to go home," she says.

The video goes to snow and that's the last image from our

Virgin Islands adventure. What you don't see is what happened after the camera faded to black.

As tired as we were, and as ready as we were to get home, we didn't get there that night. A powerful storm swept in from the east grounding all flights until the next morning. United issued us vouchers for a meal and a night's stay in a local motel, where we hunkered down and put our homecoming on hold for one more night. The storm interrupted our plans, but it didn't cancel them. There was a delay, not a termination. The wind and rain didn't dampen our desire to be in the embrace of our loved ones, it only intensified it.

Don't let the water get you down

On our journey home to heaven, there will be storms along the way. As tired as we are, and as ready as we think we are to get home, powerful storms will sweep in from nowhere and threaten to drown our faith. But, don't let the water get you down.

Waves of terror may rise in the form of suspicious X-rays, or suspicious packages in the mail; threats of eviction, or threats of divorce; FBI warnings, or cardiologist warnings; homeland security, or Social Security; loss of job or loss of health. Waves of trouble will sometimes hide the face of Christ from our view, but if we will cling to Jesus—keeping our eyes locked on Him—He won't let us drown. He will deliver us safely to the other side. He will get us home.

The storms we face are real. The lightning and sheets of water cascading from the sky that night in Chicago weren't imaginary. But we weren't about to let a little wind and water stop us from reaching our destination.

Storms can be scary. They sweep in and, this is important, *they sweep out*. That's right. Storms don't last, but home does! Routes sometimes change due to weather. Flights get rescheduled. But these are just the hassles of the journey. The final destination remains unchanged. "Weeping may endure for the night, but joy comes in the morning."

✣

Storms don't last, but home does!

As long as you have your ticket for home, you're going to arrive safely. Jesus has already paid your fare, and what's more, He's the Pilot of your plane. He's coming to get us.

ANYBODY HERE WANT OUT?

The story is told of some American prisoners of war who had been held captive by the Viet Cong somewhere in Southeast Asia. Day after day these soldiers waited and hoped for rescue, but none seemed to be coming.

Just when it seemed they would die in captivity, they heard the familiar *thump, thump, thump* of American choppers overhead. Gunfire erupted just outside their compound. Suddenly, the door to their prison exploded inward and splintered into a thousand wooden pieces. Standing in the doorway was a Rambo-like U.S. Marine with rippling muscles and rifle at the ready. He surveyed the room quickly and shouted out: "Anybody here want out?"

Jesus is coming again, my friends. Heaven's rescue party is on its way. " 'If it were not so,' " Jesus says, " 'I would have told you' " (John 14:2). He's going to "descend from heaven with a shout" (1 Thessalonians 4:16), split the sky wide open, and call out: "Anybody here want out?" "Anybody here want to go home?"

I want to go home, don't you? All signs indicate that we're almost there. If we have read and assimilated the words of Jesus, we can look out the window and see the landmarks of home. As men " 'faint from terror, apprehensive of what is coming on the world,' " (Luke 21:26); as wickedness increases and the love of most grows cold (see Matthew 24:12); as natural disasters increase in frequency and intensity (see Matthew 24:7); and as "people [become] lovers of themselves, lovers of money, boastful, proud, abusive, disobedient to their parents, ungrateful, unholy, without love, unforgiving, slanderous, without self-control, brutal, not lovers of the good, treacherous, rash, conceited, lovers of pleasure rather than lovers of God—having a form of godliness but denying its power" (2 Timothy 3:2-5), it's obvious that we've begun our descent and we must prepare for landing.

Landing is serious business. The cabin must be secured. Tray tables have to be stowed, seatbacks must be restored to their upright and locked positions. And all elec-tronic items have to be turned off.

Our Pilot, Jesus, has turned on the seat belt sign, and the time has come for us to put away our gadgets, idols, and "everything that hinders and the sin that so easily entangles" (Hebrews 12:1).

It's obvious that we've begun our descent and we must prepare for landing.

We're almost home, and it's time to get excited. It's getting bumpy on approach, and it's likely to get rougher. But "don't let your hearts be troubled." Above the drone of Anthrax reports; above the roar of bombs and cruise missiles; above the sound of weeping family members in a funeral parlor—can't you hear it? It's getting closer now. Yes, it's unmistakable.

Cheering.

Above the storm, I hear the sound of angels cheering.

They're cheering us on to victory. Don't quit. Don't lose your way now. We're about to leave this long, dark tunnel we've known as life on Planet Trouble. The welcome-home banners are being strung, and our journey is almost finished.

You know, the most you get from the airlines if you wait out a storm is a meal voucher, or at best, a free night at a decent motel. But Jesus offers so much more if we consent to "fly" with Him *through* the storms of life. No vouchers, just a promise:

" 'To him who overcomes [clings to Jesus in the storms of life] I will give the right to eat from the tree of life, which is in the paradise of God' " (Revelation 2:7).

" 'To him who overcomes [clings to Jesus in the storms of life] I will give some of the hidden manna. I will also give him a white stone with a new name written on it, known only to him who receives it' " (Revelation 2:17).

" 'To him who overcomes [clings to Jesus in the storms of life] and does my will to the end, I will give authority over the nations' " (Revelation 2:26).

" 'He who overcomes [clings to Jesus in the storms of life] . . . I will never blot out his name from the book of life, but will acknowledge his name before my Father and his angels' " (Revelation. 3:5).

" 'To Him who overcomes [clings to Jesus in the storms of life] I will make a pillar in the temple of my God. Never again will he leave it. I will write on him the name of my God and the name of the city of my God, the new Jerusalem, which is coming down out of heaven from my God; and I will also write on him my new name' " (Revelation 3:12).

" 'To him who overcomes [clings to Jesus in the storms of life] I will give the right to sit with me on my throne, just as I overcame and sat down with my Father on his throne" (Revelation. 3:21).

I can hardly wait.

❖

Lord, I want to hear You cheer for me! Please don't stop cheering me on. I want to sit with You on Your throne, and receive a new name that only You and I know about. I want to eat from the tree of life and dwell with You forever. Don't let me quit, Lord. I get so tired sometimes. Tired, distracted, and worn out with the worries of this life. But keep before me the vision of Your coming. Help me to cling to You in the storms of life, because You are certainly clinging to me. I love You, Lord. Hold my place at the table and come soon. Amen.

If you enjoyed this book, you'll enjoy these by the same author:

On Eagles' Wings
Randy Maxwell. Life can tend to weigh you down with worry, fear, and impatience. Jesus wants to help us get above our daily trials and claim victory over our difficulties. *On Eagles' Wings* offers a sensible nuts-and-bolts approach to daily Christian living that will inspire you to take action.
0-8163-1345-8. Paperback. US$4.99.

If My People Pray
Randy Maxwell. What would happen in our homes, churches, and communities if we followed God's counsel in 2 Chronicles 7:14, humbled ourselves, and prayed? This book shows how to experience prayer as relationship, power, and the key to revival.
English, 0-8163-1246-X. Paperback. US$10.99.
Spanish, 1-5755-4031-2. Paperback. US$6.99.

Bring Back the Glory
Randy Maxwell. A heart-felt look at what happens when God's people pray for revival. *Bring Back the Glory* is written for everyone who craves change and the reviving showers of blessing God longs to send—*now!*
English, 0-8163-1788-7. Paperback. US$12.99.
Spanish, 0-8163-9438-5. Paperback. US$12.99.

Order from your ABC by calling **1-800-765-6955**, or get online and shop our virtual store at **www.adventistbookcenter.com**.

- Read a chapter from your favorite book
- Order online
- Sign up for email notices on new products